MISANTHROPE

A Collection of Poems

MISANTHROPE

A Collection of Poems

By Annie Hendrix

Bardward Press

MISANTHROPE: A Collection of Poems

Copyright © 2026 ANNIE HENDRIX. All rights reserved.

Published by ANNIE HENDRIX / BARDWARD PRESS

No part of this book may be reproduced without the written permission of the author, except in the case of brief quotations in critical reviews and certain other noncommercial uses permitted by copyright law.

Cover and interior design by Jasmin Linton

Artwork by Gela Mikava

ISBN 979-8-9996689-0-5

For everyone.

> "My God! It chills my heart to see the ways
> Men come to terms with evil nowadays;
> Sometimes, I swear, I'm moved to flee and find
> Some desert land unfouled by humankind."
>
> —Molière, *The Misanthrope*

CONTENTS

PART I

When You Lose Someone You Love	2
I Walk by Candlelight	3
That Car Has No Driver	4
The Bay	5
Why Aren't You Running?	6
Traffic	7
Bicycle	8
I Am the War	9
Newsprint	10
Wings	11
Animals	12
Somewhere on Earth	13
Scroll	14
Found Poem	15
The Alley	16
Nowhere Man	17
Maple Leaves	18
Light as Air	19
Pardon Me	20
Civil War	21
Cat Calls	22
Check for Spiders	23
Nude Beach	24
Chopsticks	25
Pocket Lint	26
The Proposition	27
Seapunk	28
Come Here, Child	29
Almost	30

PART II

The Misanthrope	34
My Favorite Breakfast	35
My Secret Room	36
A Nice Little Place to Eat	37
For the Record	39
The Clarinet	40
Crone and Codger	41
At Least Once	42
Bliss	43
Floriculture	44
Flow Recovery	45
One with Nature	46
In the Yard	47
Orange River	48
The Dogs Go Wild	49
Salty Marvel	50
Gathering Glitter	51
Ground Effect	52
Mantra	53
Silence	54
Holding Space	55
Window to the World	56
The Internet	57
Leave Me Behind	58
Acknowledgments	59

MISANTHROPE

A Collection of Poems

PART I

WHEN YOU LOSE SOMEONE YOU LOVE

    have a good cry and then laugh.

Then cry again

and this time cry until you are sure
    there are no more tears,

until your clothes are sopping.

Wash the clothes and dry them well
    and be mindful of all the little blessings:

The breeze

    on your red,

        swollen eyes,

    the sun in

        your hesitant,

           curling smile.

When they ask, "How are you?"
    get lost in this impossible question,

the answer somewhere deep
    within the caverns of your grief.

Respond "I'm okay, I'm coping,"
    until you believe it

and each time you cry you'll make it true.

I WALK BY CANDLELIGHT

I walk foggy down the dusty street,
squinting past my sunglasses.
The wind is almost strong enough to keep me
from admiring the dandelions.

I ask the internet for advice,
and am greeted with an ocean
of the world selling its success to me.

Search engines help those who help themselves;
see if they open some doors for you.

Some say I am an inspiration,
but I'm a dark gelatin, a dark mass,
with a single candle cupped in my hands,
just me against the wind.

I try to keep it alight
as I walk in the night,
but sometimes
I want to let it go out.

THAT CAR HAS NO DRIVER

It has a wreath of lasers on the roof
and there is no longer room to forget
where the coffee has gone,
no space to imagine
how the hot drink flew
and splattered on the concrete.

That car has no eyes,
but it stopped as I waited on the corner
and bowed my head to an empty seat—
an empty seat!

What else does that car see
with its spinning whirring,
and what does it think
of how slowly I cross the street?

THE BAY

Some days I think of leaving,
some days she begs me to stay.

Oh, the Bay

      the Bay,

           the Bay.

WHY AREN'T YOU RUNNING?

You're wearing sneakers,

the orange laces are tied up
    so tight and I can see

you're a breath away from
    blowing it—off/up/down?

So, why aren't you running?

You're downwind of your dreams.
    If I give you just one idea

you could reach the clouds,
    pull them down, and drink!

You'll be light as flight,
    weathered as a feather—

"Get it together," *The Man* says.
    "What you're supposed to want
is halfway to where
    you're supposed to be."

So why aren't you running there?

I'm supposed to let you know,
    that's what he told me.

I'm supposed to tell on you
    when you stop.

TRAFFIC

I can fly on two wheels
as traffic flashes its
fists and fingers at me

angrily, as drivers do.

Slumped forward
over leather wheels
like melting clocks in a Dalí.

Cutting creases
deeper in their brows,
cutting corners.

BICYCLE

Rode into the night smiling,
hit a dark spot in the road,

a pocket of mist,
crossed a cat's path and slowed,

called to him, but he shied away
and I sped home.

Atoms from India, Brazil
smashed the knuckles on my bare hands

like needles,
knives in the evening chill,

as I rode into the night,
and hit a dark spot in the road.

I AM THE WAR

I breathe in and the air is still;
my last drag hangs like a flag unfurled,
peaks and valleys on the wind.

I breathe out and the birds scatter,
fly in tandem with the jets across the sky,
my blood-hot cheeks as if it were summertime
though dry autumn leaves
already mass beneath the trees.

How could I forget so easily?

I am the war.
    The war is me.

My blood boils,
    my blood is oil.

It's deafening,
    the suffering.

NEWSPRINT

Do you remember

> the world as it was,
> before the carpet bombs
> and white phosphorous?

> I don't remember.

When I was young,

> the girl who placed
> a carnation in the barrel
> of a soldier's gun

>> was already an abstraction.

WINGS

A cool café—
Cold. Blended ice,
mochas and gelato.

Indie music that lives
    primarily in the shadows,

suspended in the syrup of reverberation.

Swan in latte
    foam, art, dissociation—

> *Death of my mother*
> *death of my father*
> *death of my brother*
> *death of a nation*

(suspended in the syrup of reverberation)

    distant strings,
    birds and wings.
    I get goosebumps then.

ANIMALS

The latest horror breaks the record—

    Take shelter!

Watch them bathe, graze, carry water.
A mass grave.
Endless slaughter.

Dwell on it.

Stay safe in the cellar.
Stick together
lest we become the animals,
wallow in the white ash.

Propaganda,
trite and hollow trash.

The emperor's hands are bound.

As he beams like Miss America,
I wonder how many times
he's buried a loved one
and smiled amid the anguish,

how many times
he's cried and then laughed.

SOMEWHERE ON EARTH

A short man is grinning.
His eyes glisten,
deep pools of listening
have the hegemon
on his knees.
High intelligence.
Reverse psychology.
A game of marbles
on asphalt soaked in sun.
The planets have aligned;
of course, he has aligned them.

SCROLL

The days grow longer
and so does the list
of things to cry for.

It rolls off the table now,
a long scroll
wrapped around the room.

FOUND POEM

Imagine it:
everyone was crazy.

Even the stars were
singing in the head.

I liked it in a funny way,
and I was not afraid.

THE ALLEY

Brick after brick
stacked in a row,
simple masonry
taken for granted.

> *How are these hands supposed to build a life*
> *if they don't know how?*

We are all such individuals,
multifaceted stones.
None of us fits
until we wield the chisel.

> *Last time I tried to change someone*
> *they ended up dead.*

I want nothing more than to let go
I can't see the sky anymore
without crying.

> *Why are my hands so cold?*

Through the shimmer and the haze,
I toil away
brick by brick,
row by row.

NOWHERE MAN

There are things I can't get past

little snags,
    sharp catches
rip my pants.

I'm afraid they'll see what's hidden
underneath my mask.

Mad sketches,
    hard edges,
nowhere fast.

MAPLE LEAVES

The maple leaves have turned brown,
fresh mulch on matted pine,
a curved moon dips in the sky.

The cotton boll stings,
and the wool over your eyes
is soft enough to believe

and just do,
and just do.

You could spend all your life
walking toward something
and away from yourself,

the night owl coos,
the night owl coos.

You keep sketching your life in charcoal
in case you need to undo yourself
after you've lost your spark
and are no longer green and dreaming.

Maybe your leaves have just turned brown,
maybe your hope is dormant now.

LIGHT AS AIR

I am heavy on the ground,
but I want to be light—
light as air

Yet I'm tethered
by tangled strands of flesh,
misaligned.

I feel bad about how often I feel bad,
about how often I feel
light as air—

I know I can do better
and I am,
and I am.

PARDON ME

Greetings from limbo.
I'm floating between islands of knowing.

I've seen too much,
the scalloped layers hot to touch—

cord taut, full of rot,
nerves shot, head down,
walk the street, stare at my feet.

Bah- dah- dum,
bah- dah- dum,
bah- dah- dum

Draped in salmon cotton,
I break up the twisted sheets of fascial adhesion.
My hands are so full of myself,
the fused bands of muscle remember

death's merciful pardon.

I have sold my body—
not as a prostitute,
but I have sold my body.

I learned the hard way,
the cannibalism of labor
can hollow you out

and I'm worth nothing unfed.

Have I learned yet,
not to break myself
just to prove myself unbreakable?

That I am better soft than dead?

CIVIL WAR

Today my body's soft beneath the skin,
my bones blanketed by
quieted tissue on the mend.

Each cell is peaceful,
the way it must have been
a long, long time ago
before the civil war began.

CAT CALLS

Out the gate, dodged a pack of tiny strays.
Seven blocks to the train.
Sky and chipper, I'm all bark in my red mini,
all laces and legs.
I pound the concrete
and puff past a man swaggering,
all fedora and blaze,
who can't keep his mouth shut.

I expect some rapacious, crass speech act
as he holds me in his gaze
he says, "If God had made anything better,"
then smokes his grass,
"He would have kept it for himself,"
and leaves me in the high of his wake,
all taken and blank

as he trips into the corner store
the cat calls back,
"If God had made anything better
He would have kept it for himself!"

CHECK FOR SPIDERS

Check for spiders under the lamp,
on the ceiling.

Everywhere.

How do you get a zip tie off
without a knife?

The stars are listening
to strangers fucking.

NUDE BEACH

I want to lie flat and naked on a rock
but this nude beach is a watering hole
and I am the prey.

Water rushes around the rocks,
so large and round
I want to hold them in my arms.

I can't be left alone by anything here.
The wasps lick the salt from my skin,
and as I sit at water's edge—
    Something makes a sound, a mad dash for my sandwich!
Ground squirrel almost got away with it, too.

Every man is first a voice,
then a shiny naked bald head,
and then a smaller, naked bald head.

The beach is nude and so is he,
and I would be too if his eyes weren't on me.

CHOPSTICKS

We went to Hawaii for a wedding.
I didn't know Honolulu had a Chinatown,
you didn't know how to use chopsticks.

I laughed too loud
when the waitress insisted you stop trying.
"You need a fork," she said,
and your face turned red
as the calliandra we'd seen
that day in the botanic garden.

I told you the powder-puff blooms near the waterfall
reminded me of the bottlebrush flower
my first love picked for me one summer.

I didn't know you'd be so jealous of a memory.
You didn't know I wouldn't marry you.

POCKET LINT

I shoved you off like a sweater on a hot night,
hoping that blankets would hold me close
and that skin against skin, all my own,
would feel like

        another you.

I left you like a plate at a diner
for a pretty waitress to carry away
and cleanse of all the oily crumbs I left behind.

I left you like a fingerprint,
like pocket lint,
like pieces of rock and flint in sand.

THE PROPOSITION

I want to tell you about the waterfall,
but if I keep my secrets

you'll keep your fingers
wrapped around that stone.

SEAPUNK

There is a current running out my eyes,
    blowing like Sahara dust
      across the dunes and slacks.

There is a hint of green in your reply.
    I see it—
    wish I didn't sometimes.

Yeah, I know we were looking for blue.
    I know underneath the concrete
        the roaches and snails congregated
    and conspired against our faith,
and the octopi recoiled
    when I pulled free from the dirt;
        wrapped in sea foam and thunder,
    I sank my teeth into a writhing fish,
grew legs, and learned to breathe.

Still, although I've been rockin' the legs for a while,
    I miss my tail,
    and fishnet on my fingers,
    and shells in my hair, I do.

    I miss my scales.

Land critters, pssshhh—
I've got better things to do than
prance around like some demigod.

    So drown me.
    Bury me in mud.

You know I can't take the heat.

COME HERE, CHILD

I see your eyes are red from crying,
your fair skin blotched,
I smell cigarettes and scotch on your breath,
and you look at me,
a child grown old from waiting.

If only you knew how beautiful you are,
crumpled like Van Gogh on the museum floor,
you'd put out your worries and doubts
and that cigarette.

Forgive and forget.
Forgive yourself for all you have and haven't done.
Now, while you're young
and have the world up your sleeve.

For years you've looked at your own reflection
and haven't seen it,
fishing for cardinal tetras in the Bering Sea
when really you are an angelfish.

ALMOST

I dreamt again last night I saw my mother,
this time standing on the cliffside at Bodega Head
overlooking the rock near where we lowered her urn.

The spray glittered in the evening sun.
The sea lions were singing again.
She almost looked back at me, almost.

PART II

THE MISANTHROPE

Maybe I'll spill over with love.
Poppies open up,
seed pods burst and give without end
so I will, too.

Maybe I'll learn love green as a child's,
sweet as spring is soft and wild,
hot as summer is dry and blue.

Maybe my love
doesn't break things beyond repair,
but catalyzes change;
flowers bloom everywhere.

MY FAVORITE BREAKFAST

                        eggs
                   scrambled
             fried or poached
           topped with cheese
               and avocado
                    on toast

MY SECRET ROOM

I ran barefoot toward the setting sun,
rays cast across the wild wheat,
covered with wet plumes
of frothy spit bug spittle.
My hands so soft and little
ripped the seed heads from the grasses
while my brothers pulled the weeds from the root.

I was strong enough to climb the pruner's rope
left idle in the cypress tree,
and clambered to the top
of my secret room in the canopy
to gaze at the Western sun
as it draped the grazing horses, cows, and sheep
in golden sheets of whatever light is made of

and I didn't wonder who created this heaven,
this sparkling field of grass and dew
because no one had told me about God
but I knew I had opened a window
and all I had to do was let it in.

A NICE LITTLE PLACE TO EAT

At the café in Glen Park
the man behind the counter
prepares to make
croissant French toast
by washing his hands
and putting on Louis Armstrong.

>   The butter on the pan
>   sizzles beneath
>   the scrape and crash
>   of the spatula swing,
>   whip of the whisk,
>   hum of the espresso machine.

Even as I wipe
other people's crumbs
off the wooden table,
I can only be grateful
this man is alive—

>   dipped in egg and fried,
>   covered in flecks
>   of powdered sugar
>   and cinnamon.

While the late
Louis's trumpet laments
"St. James Infirmary Blues"
he and my mother
both speak from the grave.

I hear Louis say
"Let her go, let her go God bless her,"
and I hear my mother say
she would have loved
>   the stained glass,
>   local art display
>   masking a jagged
>   hole in the wall,
>   recycled burlap
>   chipped paint—

Had she not been taken
to the grave when she was,
how many more years
would she have loved?

FOR THE RECORD

I love jazz.

The sizzle and the crash,
the stacked harmonics
of the easy shuffle sing.

My voice is not needed,
the subvocal grunts
are enough to swing, so

Can I get a chorus
up front while I drink?

Y'all think the bass plays
slave to the changes,
but bass is king.

While the keys comp,
the horns bop, and the sax
laughs as it screams.

These angels,
these agents of culture
load America's music
into the club and out again
at 2AM when no one's around
but the drunks and the club owner.

They don't do it for you.
They don't do it for the money.
They do it for the *shoo- bee- doo- bee.*

I love all of it, and "All of You,"
and "All of Me," for the record.

I love jazz.

THE CLARINET

My husband plays clarinet in the bedroom,
and I await the sound of round air
forced through the bell and keys.

Each controlled exhalation vibrates the reed
as the ongoing waves ripple and squeeze
under the door.

Only my most sensitive bits of tissue
respond to the wet, percussive articulation of his tongue;
tympanic membranes are among
the fragile flesh impressed by his clarity of tone.

His lips make my attempts at recorded song
feel like a mockery of pleasure,
yet I carry on.

CRONE AND CODGER

A crone in a windbreaker
kneels amid the ice plant
like a maiden in superbloom.

Behind the camera lens
a codger captures her
alive on the coastal bluff.

She is on her knees
for no reason other than
to press her lined palms
to the vivid green.

He takes her portrait,
she gives him a leaf.

AT LEAST ONCE

I'm happy every day at least once,
at least as happy as I was that summer
when it was raining in Berlin,
and we were absolutely done with each other.

My handlebars were crooked,
your wheel hub bent half to hell,
ruined by what I had done
on the run from California.

I cobbled the parts
as if I were some kind of mechanic,
as if we weren't manic and young
with just a semblance of a plan,
as if the cobblestones and panic
wouldn't shatter us.

We laughed as we shouted past
our pink gums and white enamel
as if we weren't yelling at each other
for the last time by the River Spree.

We pretended we'd get through the rain
and everything would go back to how it was.
The locals didn't give a damn about the storm
as we sprinted from the train to the bus.

Fourteen years have passed
and still, I remember the chain lube on my hands
and every time I did too much.
I swear, I loved you every day at least once.

BLISS

Bliss is waking up in the groggy afternoon.
Sticky thighs and fingers kiss,
damp hairs lick as if possessed
by a will all their own.

I groan,
peel my eyelids half-open
and see your own
still twitching with dreams.

How sweet, I think.
Our noses bridging,
lips almost kissing
in the silence of sleep.

I lay still and breathe with you
like ocean waves lapping the beach,
and I can't help but disturb this peace
for want of more.

FLORICULTURE

Your hands stimulate floriculture,
your body more than a machine.

We conserve our sacred pleasure,
by pinching off the legacy.

Some misunderstand the simple life,
seek purple berries large and juicy.

Compatible neighbors bloom together,
indifferent to pomology.

Strong attachments made from scratch
need repair and restoration

best to tend the substrate
so the intercourse can last forever.

FLOW RECOVERY

The river runs in both directions
at the confluence,

erosion tricks the eye
and water runs skyward.

Stagnation forces flow
into holy embrace,

deep oscillations
interface;

becoming One
is rhythmically unstable.

Each begs the other
to shed the shear layers

and reach
maximum velocity.

ONE WITH NATURE

One day my husband will senesce,
white-haired and red-necked,
bald head among the leaves,
nose deep in the redbud tree.

I will love him, I will love that
he loved himself enough to care
for the pithy cartilage of his body.
Will he say the same of me?

Will he die surrounded by love
second only to our own?
Oh, how my husband loves
pruning the redbud tree.

IN THE YARD

In the yard there are more robins
than I have ever seen.

The river rises and pools
around every stone.

A squirrel descends the bitter orange—
Looks like the half-eaten fruit
at the base of the trunk is his!

Neon juice against the mud
and fallen liquidambar leaves

This is enough
this is enough for me.

ORANGE RIVER

Orange River crept up again overnight.
Now trapped water winds around the stones.
Fallen oranges litter the soil,
ornaments on the mulch.

The saturated sky
sun-dances behind the clouds,
and as the wind whirls around
each leaf is moved.

Blue light washes over massed shapes
like varnish on wood,
water on stones,
wax on apples.

The Granny Smith buds out
and soon there may be too many apples
for the young branches to bear.

Overhead a severed limb sprouts
in spite of itself:
the rejected offspring
of the elder liquidambar tree.

The plum, in her old age,
still manages to feed
a few ivory flowers
into the glistening fountain.

Cool blue illusion,
light diffusion.

THE DOGS GO WILD

Look toward the sky.
What's up there?

Everything hope,
everything despair.

Beneath, surfers
slick as seals

ride the crossing waves.
Ascending white noise

        percolates;

there is no panic
in this undulating sound

but the kinetic turbulence
makes the dogs go wild.

SALTY MARVEL

The ocean waves forgive all,
eternal fountain of youth
breaks all things down,
makes all things new.

Our half naked bodies
walk the shore,
shape the fragile dunes.

Endless sparkle,
salty marvel.

There are wooden structures
all along the jagged coast
sitting and waiting
for the sleeper waves.

>   My smile's tight against my face.
>   I laugh into the salt spray,
>   dip my hands in the foam
>
>   as the wake beckons,
>   the sea threatens
>   to take me into the whole.

I lie on the sand,
and from my hands
pour warm waterfalls
of the ancient.

GATHERING GLITTER

Months after the plastic
baubles hit the shelves,

weeks after we laughed
at how big the skeletons

have gotten, how early
they emerged this year,

the autumn leaves are falling
from the liquidambar tree.

It's one hundred degrees,
but this is no desert.

Once our rivers overflowed,
before the flood of concrete

cured the oak woodland
of anything but us,

the saturated valley floor
masqueraded as a lake.

The Maidu didn't spend
this dry, transitional time

gathering glitter for
their glyphosatic lawns,

but rather preparing to ascend
the foothills to get

every acorn not yet
hidden by the birds.

GROUND EFFECT

The blank page
is endless in front of me,
its waters undisturbed.

This kind of perfection
can't be helped by writing,
it can only be ruined,
and I am the ruiner.

The splash of the ink on the page
makes ripples and streaks
like a bird flying low
near the surface of the lake,
dipping her pointed claw in just a little,
dropping feathers.

I could say I am that bird,
but it would be boastful.
The threshold between
humans and nature
grows ever stronger,
and I am only human
I'm not capable
of such tender beauty
as that made by birds.

This humbles me,
as does the realization
that this pen is not a claw,
this page is not a pond,
and so I am free to ruin it.

MANTRA

I am the rushing river,
I am the force that flows.
Not the leaf that floats and flitters
nor the passive stone.

SILENCE

I pray to the silence.
I pray to the emptiness
from which I came,
to which I'll return.

The stars sit in silence,
in deep velvet luxury
from which I came,
to which I'll return again.

I find in the silence,
I find in the emptiness,
a most extraordinary feeling
only told by silence.

HOLDING SPACE

When I listen to what's inside,
I remember the brushing grass,
the whispering leaves,

and the soft wind
plays my ear
like a hollow flute.

There is a sense of not knowing,
an empty cup,
and I must fill it up with aspirations.
I must.

Deeper down there is a hunger,
a longing to keep it empty,
to bathe in the dark nothing
of true quiet.

But my hands sweat
when I think about
the discomfort of holding space

as the soft wind
plays my ear
like a hollow flute.

WINDOW TO THE WORLD

Look through this window,
Window to the Whole World!
Through it I see what you see,
my own life peripheral.

I can almost smell the surf,
the heat of the sun beating down your eyelids.
Today I don't have to squint,
I'm couchbound and shielded from any kind of weather.

While I double tap
you listen to a gentle rainstorm,
kiss the evening breeze,
laugh into the sky.

It's so easy to share my love this way.

THE INTERNET

You think this place is a portal to the infinite,
a door to the unknown.
You create ghosts
and send them into the machine.

Outside the Earth heaves
as our bodies slouch and groan.
The great rift grows wide—

       tectonic eruption!

Crack and slide.

You think you have bridged the tenth dimension?
Just remember you can come back!
The door is always open to the feeling world.

Close your eyes.

Your heart can open itself.
You can touch the soul
of another human being

       universes collide.

LEAVE ME BEHIND

I don't want to disappear,
but I don't fit into that architecture.

I'll stay behind
and tend to the tender things.

ACKNOWLEDGMENTS

My deepest appreciation goes to:

BILL BAYNES
for mentorship and critical feedback on this collection of poems

JOSHUA LAVENDER
for careful editing

JASMIN LINTON
for devoted design work

GELA MIKAVA
for donation of the artwork *The Abstract Face in Pink and Green*

VĀNEÇKA
for helping choose the final cover design

SUSAN KORN AND ALL THE MEMBERS OF GOLD COUNTRY WRITERS
for encouragement, connection and community

MY DEAR READERS ON SUBSTACK
for enthusiastic engagement with my work

TRAVIS W. HENDRIX
for loving me for exactly who I am

"Silence" was released as a musical setting of the same name on *Folkish*, an album of original songs, in 2020.

"One with Nature" first appeared in the anthology *Vision & Verse: A Fusion of Poetry, Prose, Art, and Photography* by California Writers Club in 2024.

www.ingramcontent.com/pod-product-compliance
Lightning Source LLC
Chambersburg PA
CBHW030448100526
44580CB00002B/34